Unlock Your Potential

Know Your Brain and How It Works

Dr. Margaret A. Golton

FRANK PUBLICATIONS   *New York*

Acknowledgments

Responsibility for the content and format of what follows is mine and mine alone. There are, however, a few people to whom I am profoundly indebted and for whose interest I am deeply grateful: Nicholas L. King for having spotted my wings and encouraged me to fly; Francoise Bartlett for her guidance and generous assessment; Ben G. Frank for his unfaltering confidence, his promotion, and his persistent prodding for clarity, precision, and specifics; Robert Kopelman for his excellent art and design of this book; and Bonita Vargo for her dedication and expertise in preparing the manuscript for publication.

How fortunate I am to have had them on my team. They have made this writing an exciting adventure. I hope both the excitement and the adventure will reach those who risk these pages.

Library of Congress Cataloging in Publication Data

Golton, Margaret A.
    Unlock your potential.

    Bibliography: p.
    1. Brain. 2. Intellect. I. Title.
QP376.G66   153   82-2490
ISBN 0-942952-00-6   AACR2

Produced by Olivestone Publishing Services
Printed in the United States of America

Published by
Frank Publications
60 East 42nd St.
Suite 757
New York, N.Y. 10017

Contents

Preface

INTRODUCTION   1

Chapter I   **Mental Health: A Model   5**

Philosophical Guidelines   7
Personality Requisites   9

Chapter II   **The Brain: Organization and Design   13**

The Brain: The Anatomy of It   13
Evolutionary History   14

Chapter III   **The Predesigned (Primitive) Brain: Its Operational Format   21**

The Limbic Section: Life and Longing   22
Limbic Inadequacy and Power Abuse   22
Knowledge Checklist: The Limbic Section   27
The Right Hemisphere: Wings and Worries   35

Chapter IV   **The Postprimitive Brain: Line of Authority   38**

The Left Hemisphere: "Let's Look at the Facts"   38
Demands: Left Hemisphere on Limbic Section   39
Demands: Left Hemisphere on Right Hemisphere   41
The Neural Sheath: The Executive Branch   43
The Executive "I": The Final Authority   44
A Revolt   45
Organizational Realities   48

Chapter V   **Orchestration: The Brain in Concert   50**

Procedures for Orchestration   52
Requisites for Change   58
Furrowing Mental Soil   60
Points to Ponder   62
Summary   64

Chapter VI   **A New Agenda   66**

Current Reality and Future Projections   69
Redesigning to "Live"   70
To Make Life "Better"   70
To Have Life Be Different   72
Addendum   76
References   76
Bibliography   76

Preface

What difference does it make? Does it make a difference if:

Individual brains are organized differently?
The neural network predesigned by nature is simple or complex?
There is in the predesigned brain *only one* center of control through which stimuli are channeled?

These are questions which brain research findings have been raising since the 1960s. Arriving at definitive answers will require further investigation and time. But we can make a beginning.

Unlock Your Potential: Know Your Brain and How It Works is such a beginning. The aim of this book is threefold: (1) to whet your curiosity as you view those who make up your world as though you have never seen them before; (2) to encourage personal exploration—to look at yourself as though you have never seen "you" before; and (3) to challenge you to action—to make the most of who you are and who you can be.

Brain research findings hold out new hope that the human species, magnificent as it is, will not only survive but will prosper in today's changing world of ever-unfolding opportunities and challenges.

University Heights, Ohio   M.A.G.
March 1982

Introduction

"No situation is so good that it cannot be better." She lived by this motto. With it she turned my professional life around as I entered the thirteenth year of my work experience. She was not a perfectionist. Far from it. She was an expansionist where human potential was concerned. The once popular song "You can be better than you are / You can be swinging on a star" could have been her theme song as she pondered the uniqueness of each individual whose life she touched.

She looked to her staff for questions that needed to be answered and for answers that needed to be questioned. Under her leadership the wartime day care center we developed was rated one of the best in the country, a model for others to follow. There was a rarity about her. She knew we didn't have all the answers. Furthermore, she had both the temerity and the humility to suggest that we didn't even have all the questions. What a legacy she left the brain cells of my mind!

The wide open spaces of the world and the human personality to which she unlocked the doors for me have been a driving force in my persistent search for the basics and the universals in human experience.

This book is a culmination of over forty years of professional practice distilled through personal trauma, examined under the psychological microscope provided by current findings in brain research. It is up-to-date. The concepts and theories it presents have been tested in my clinical practice over the past three years. The results have been dramatic. They have been replicated in a wide range of situations and have proven firm. My aim here is to make public a new approach to mental health.

This new approach is based on findings in brain research since 1960. It deals with brain organization and neural network design. The procedures it uses are based on the assumption that the brain, like all other organs of the human system, has certain in-born characteristics. It is also equipped with the capacity to develop and change.

Implicit in what follows is the conviction that the human organism is subject to the three basic laws of nature: (1) the law of gravity or inertia, (2) the law of conservation, and (3) the law of magnetism. These laws operate in all human beings, albeit with different levels of intensity in different individuals and in different circumstances.

Two conditions are essential for effecting change in brain organization and neural network design in the light of the three basic laws of nature: (1) desire for change and (2) determination to achieve change whatever the cost in time, energy, or commitments.

The desire and the determination must be firm. Because the demands are great, willingness to pay the price psychologically, socially, and physically must be without qualification. The end results are well worth the price. This statement, however, one must take on faith, because one can know its truth only after the results have been achieved. Models—individuals who have "made it"—provide the incentive. They give objective evidence of the "promise." Models are necessary, at least at the beginning of the enterprise.

Though models are extremely effective, concepts and theories are also important. They provide anchorage and perspective. They can serve as checkpoints and guidelines so that individuals can consider what is valid for themselves, what is incompatible with their frame of reference and their own values.

Undergirding this approach is faith that nature's intent is for a better world, a world suited to the needs, wishes, and dreams of human beings operating at the very highest level of their potential. Nature is elitist, but it is not exclusive in its elitism. While it promotes the survival of the fittest, it has equipped the human organism with a brain that carries for each individual the potential for being among the fittest. Like the recently discovered underground rivers of the earth that have neither source nor outlet, human potential remains to be explored.

It is intriguing to view the human brain as one does a fine musical instrument: something to be explored for quality and scope; something to be practiced and exercised. There seems to be hope and challenge in realizing that the brain can be reorganized and redesigned if one is not satisfied with the organization and design provided by nature. Such a revamping is not easy. But it can be done. There are simple procedures to aid one in the task.

What is presented here is most likely to appeal to those who want things better—the quality seekers; and those who want things different—the inventors. In the promise and the procedures is an invitation to each individual to plumb the reaches of his or her hidden resources and to mobilize them for effective living in an ever-expanding world.

CHAPTER 1

Mental Health: A Model

"If you don't know where you're going, any road will get you there," it has been said. Mental health is a specific destination. Not just any road will get us there. One of the many problems that plague us is that the characteristics of our destination are complex. How much easier it is to know when something is wrong than when something is as it should be. One young woman put it well: "Things are good. I want them to be great." What is "good"? What is "great"? These are subjective qualities. They are conditions that vary with time, place, and people. They are not constants.

Cynthia had never had any question that she would "make it." She had been a beautiful, adored only child. At age five she directed and starred in her own plays, to the delight of her playmates and the adults in her life. As a beauty queen and cheerleader she had many friends who seemed to enjoy her glory and find their reflection in it.

It was no surprise that after five years on her first job, Cynthia was promoted to an administrative position in a large advertising concern. It was certainly no surprise to Cynthia. She had worked hard. She knew her goal was within reach.

Something was missing. Something was different. Co-workers and colleagues admired her, respected her, and cooperated. But they did not adore her or show her the same kind of affection that she had known in the past. There were times, in fact, when the climate felt frigid. She found herself feeling alone in a sense she had never experienced before.

In her steady, upward climb she had not learned that adults who use their capabilities fully may stir envy and even hostility in other people. To have others share in the enjoyment of her success and in her moving ahead, she might need to team up with other achievers. In other words, she may have to develop a "psychological family."

As we undertake to define "mental health," the most we can hope to do is to set forth some general criteria. Each criterion is like a grain of sand, a universe in itself encompassing values, priorities, and goals.

The following analysis aims to provide some benchmarks, much as surveyors do as they chart terrain. Where mental health is concerned, each benchmark is subject to in-depth consideration by each participant in this mental health expedition. Individuals must decide which and to what extent each benchmark applies to themselves. The criteria offered here are not absolutes. They will be conditioned by each individual's values, priorities, and goals. Essentially, the following discussion reflects my own values, priorities, and goals as they have been distilled over many years of living, research, study, and clinical practice. They have provided guidelines. They have stood up well in a long lifetime.

I was a junior in college. My psychology professor was in one of his usual philosophical moods. Wisdom was often subtly interwoven with scientific findings on personality. "We do not have to justify our reason for being," he mused soberly. "All God wants of us is that we enjoy life."

Enjoy life? Somehow as all of us struggled with the realities of a collapsed economy, survival, not enjoyment, was the order of the day. Work and responsibility had been the themes I had grown up on as an only child, a first-generation American. In the words of Longfellow: "Life was real; life was earnest. . . ." Another dimension to this philosophy was added on another occasion:

We'd be in less danger
Of the wiles of a stranger
If our own kin and kith
Were more fun to live with.

"Fun"—a safeguard against danger—this too was new. Both messages were deeply ingrained in my mind. It is even possible that they have served as the pillars around which I have woven my life. I have certainly passed them on to the many people with whom I have worked clinically over many years. They seem somehow to thrust the concept of life into a very special perspective, to give it a very special connotation.

Enjoying and having fun, however, have their own unique characteristics. As we view people and how they live their lives, we might fairly assume that the capacity for these experiences does not come with the genes. They may well be abilities which we need to develop through practice.

Philosophical Guidelines

In the philosophical treasure chest we have inherited from those who have preceded us we find observations, instructions, suggestions, directions, warnings—wisdom accumulated through the ages. These guidelines and these guide-posts can provide the psyche with the nurturance necessary for fruitful living.

> "If at first you don't succeed, try, try again" conveys the message that the human organism is emergent. The fact that it cannot do something today does not mean that it will not be able to tomorrow. The crucial issue is perseverance, commitment to the task.

> "God helps those who help themselves" speaks to transcendance, the awareness that there are forces beyond our control and beyond our comprehension, which may be available to us in our struggles.

> "If it is to be, it is up to me" affirms our separateness, our innate integrity (wholeness, soundness) and ultimately our self-authority to do or not to do, to be or not to be.

> "Happy are those who dream dreams and are ready to pay the price to make them come true" attests to the importance of imagining the life you would like to live. Goals perhaps, but not necessarily. "Dreams" can be images of experiences that would interest, enrich, or challenge, not with any specific intent except the enjoying of life.

The German philosopher Goethe said: "As soon as you trust yourself, you will know how to live." The English writer Rudyard Kipling developed the issue of trust in his poem "If." But he cast the matter into the social arena:

> If you can keep your head when all about you
> Are losing theirs and blaming it on you.
> If you can trust yourself when all men doubt you,
> And make allowance for their doubting too. . . .

To trust oneself and especially to trust oneself in the face of the doubt of others requires a firm sense of self—of one's separateness, of one's wholeness—and also clarity as to one's values, priorities, and goals. There must not only be a "you." There must be an "authentic" you, a you ready and willing to stand up and be counted. An interesting "go ahead" was sounded by a modern observer (Robert Talbert): "Blow your own horn. You're the only one who knows the tune."

Personality Requisites

Mental health requires a reasonably accurate perception of reality. "Life is like an onion," wrote poet Carl Sandburg, "you peel it off one layer at a time, and sometimes you weep." One must guard against the Pollyanna stance: "Things happen for the best." This is not necessarily so. What is true and without qualification is that one must make the best of what happens if one is to "live." Robert Louis Stevenson offered some truly challenging advice: "Keep your doubts to yourself; share your courage." What an opportunity to make available to others one's strength. There is, in fact, the possibility that strength, like happiness, is contagious; that both are reflections of the third basic law of nature, the law of magnetism.

The law of magnetism has had little support in the Western world these last few hundred years. One philosopher has observed that as scientific advances have brought within reach a world suited to the needs of people, human beings have become preoccupied with doom and disaster. In the realm of economics, we have assigned more of our resources to weapons of destruction than to the building of a peaceful, humane world through the development of human psychological potential. These are distressing observations. They are potentially disastrous as far as the survival of the human species is concerned.

"Miracles sometimes occur," said Chaim Weizmann, "but one has to work terribly hard for them." In an age of massive and rapid social change miracles are not likely to happen by spontaneous mutations or evolutionary spurts. They will come as a result of consciousness of need and deliberateness of purpose. In this connection there are a number of lessons we can learn from the turtle, among the oldest of living organisms. The turtle has survived whereas the dinosaur has not, in spite of its awesome physique. Approximately 300 million years ago the turtle learned to live on land as well as in water. It prefers water but it can survive on land.[1]

Like the turtle, human beings living in a mobile, global society may have to adapt. They may have to be able to live with relationships or without them. They may have to learn to make the most of relationships on the run, finding significance and beauty in the ships that pass in the night, fleeting in time but lasting in effect.

Another lesson humans may learn from the turtle is that the creature moves ahead only when it sticks out its neck.

The turtle's environment is different from that of the human being. Its biological equipment is also dramatically different. As far as we know, there is nothing that the turtle has done in its world that is equivalent to what human beings have done in theirs: ten numerical digits—1 to 10—have made it possible to go to the moon and back; from 26 letters of the alphabet the English language alone has emerged into a system of 400,000 words. It has been estimated that there are 140 languages on earth. Out of seven musical notes—do, re, mi, fa, so, la, ti—have come symphonies and operas. The potential of the human brain is beyond the brain's comprehension.

Imagination. Adventure. Discovery. These human endeavors will lead us to achieving human potential. To exercise imagination, to risk adventure, to commit oneself to discovery requires openness, flexibility, wonder, curiosity, and, above all, conviction about and commitment to the principle that the human personality is emergent.

With this psychological equipment we may be able to engage the life experience with the enthusiasm of a tourist in a country rich in history and varied in culture. This is an "all eyes and ears" approach to each day, each experience. Perhaps then life can be addressed as the miracle that it is, to be experienced, not understood; to be valued and cherished.

For mental health one must be free of control by automatic, random, and instinctive impulses. All human behavior must be under the control of the conscious, rational mental processes rooted in knowledge, reason, and reality. An internal psychological hub strong enough to withstand the uneven terrain of living is an essential. There must also be safeguards against venturing unnecessarily and fruitlessly onto the rough terrain on which others find themselves. Too often we find in the distress of others refuge from life's challenges. It is not easy to achieve a balance—between what one gives others and what one holds on to zealously for oneself. To be able to set limits to giving without feeling selfish, without feeling guilty, and without worrying that one may be invoking the wrath of the gods requires:

A sense of time—everyone has only one life to live.

Clarity on rights—each individual has the right to live life as fully as is possible within the limits of unalterable realities.

Clarity on obligations. Two criteria are helpful here: What can you live with? What adds to your good feeling about yourself—to your self-esteem?

Confidence in and commitment to the future—a sense of one's inalienable right to live, to be free, and to engage in pursuit of happiness, whatever that might be.

It is helpful if one can displace fear with knowledge and skill; if for envy one can substitute dedication without ambition; if the only person with whom one is in competition is oneself. Every living organism comes genetically equipped for survival. Potential comes in the rough, like the diamond deeply embedded in coal. Potentials must be located. A conscious decision must be made as to which are to be mined and developed. The process is not automatic. Developing one's potentials requires effort, energy, and determination. It is the surest road to mental health.

CHAPTER 2

The Brain: Organization and Design

Technology has put us in command of our environment. The compass, for example, made it possible for us to circle the earth; the telescope opened the heavens to exploration. Perhaps knowledge of the brain will put us in command of our needs, wishes, and dreams so that external and internal potential can be brought together in the best interest of nature and human nature.[2]

The Brain: The Anatomy of It

The human brain: its cells and neural fibers weigh only three and one-half pounds. Computerized, its content would completely fill Carnegie Hall. So estimates Peter Russell as he considers what he describes as the "most evolved system" on this planet, a system that is the spearhead of evolution.[3] Only since the 1960s have we had the instruments necessary to begin to study how the brain functions. Brain research is now at the frontier of science. Scientists from many different disciplines are engaged in this area of exploration.

Evolutionary History

Visualize the brain as diamond-shaped. Segment the lowest angle to include one-fifth of the organ. This is the limbic section, the oldest portion of the brain (approximately three million years old), often designated as the reptilian brain because its equivalent is found in reptiles. The limbic section is the seat of emotional behavior: love, hate, anger, passion, aggression. It is the site of the autonomic nervous system, which governs breathing, hunger, circulation.

Next in evolutionary seniority is the right hemisphere (approximately two and one-half million years old). The right hemisphere has both visual and auditory capacity (dreams). It is the source of imagination. It can sing but not speak. It can write poetry but not rhyme. It is a master at spatial relationships and math.

Equal in size but much younger in evolutionary history is the left hemisphere. Physiological anthropologists believe that the left hemisphere came into existence approximately 300,000 years ago when the brain doubled in size. The left hemisphere accumulates knowledge and has a keen sense of time, sequence, and reality. It is the source of logic, judgment, and reason. It can speak but not sing.

Covering the top of the right and left hemispheres like a blanket is a narrow sheath of neural fibers.[4] This area is probably the youngest part of the brain. It may be responsible for the "origin of consciousness," which Julian Jaynes dates to having taken place only about 3,000 years ago.[5] From the activity taking place here one may assume that it is the locus of the ego. It is the part of the brain where the decisions are made as to which stimuli go where. In this neural sheath would be what Sigmund Freud called the guardian or the gatekeeper, the selecting-directing mechanism. In this area of the brain lie values, priorities, goals, the guidelines for stimuli distribution.

Over and above the neural sheath in authority is the executive "I," the core of the individual personality, often referred to as the "will." The executive "I" gives direction to the neural sheath. It is essentially the source of values, priorities, and goals.

The brain, with its sections ranging in age from 3,000 to 5,000 years for the neural sheath to three million years for the limbic section, with the left hemisphere in between at 300,000 years, might be viewed as a two-generational family. The limbic section and the right hemisphere might be viewed as being of the same generation, for there is only a 500,000-year span between them. More than two million years elapsed between the evolution of the right hemisphere and the left hemisphere. Along with the difference in age is a marked difference in how the two sections function. The limbic section and the right hemisphere seem to be governed solely by nature's predesign, by instinct, reflex, and habit. These areas have no concern with knowledge, reality, time, or sequence. The left hemisphere, on the other hand, is concerned with reality and time, with knowledge, logic, and judgment. The emergence of the neural sheath added a dimension to left hemisphere functioning in its concern with values, priorities, and goals. The neural sheath is a directional aid to the left hemisphere's search for what is and why, for what can be and how it can be made to be.

Freud and his contemporaries spoke of the fact that human beings had more than one brain and that often the various brains were in collusion with one another against the best interests of the individual. According to the *International Encyclopedia of Psychiatry, Psychology, and Neurology* (1977), the most firmly established findings of modern neurology are those related to hemisphere specialization.[6] In 1953 Roger Sperry of the California Institute of Technology discovered that if the corpus callosum, a thin bridge of tissue which connects the right and left hemispheres of the brain, is severed, the individual is left with two minds, or two separate spheres of consciousness, each independent of and indifferent to the other.

Noam Chomsky, a researcher at the Massachusetts Institute of Technology, has suggested that the human mind is "a set of separate mental organs," each as "distinct and as faithful to its own rules of operation as the heart, liver and eye." The connecting link is the corpus callosum. Consisting of an incalculable number of neuron fibers, the corpus callosum keeps each hemisphere in touch with what is going on in the other hemisphere.[7] It is when each section functions in harmony with the values, priorities, and goals of the executive "I" under the director in the neural sheath (executive office) that the individual functions maximally.

We now have objective evidence that brains are predesigned. Some people are born with brains containing an intricate network of neural fibers. Others are born with brains that have a simple network design. Some of the neural networks have many points of connection; others, only a few. In some brains there are many centers of control through which stimuli are channeled. In others there is only a single center of control through which all stimuli are channeled. Possibly persons whom we characterize as one-track-minded are individuals with only one center of control. We have tended to assume that such people were rigidly toilet trained or subjected to single-minded training. These assumptions may not be true. The culprit may be neural network design over which neither the individual nor his or her nurturers had any control or the knowledge necessary to modify.

To summarize, among the most important of the research findings are the following:

1. The brain is plastic. It is impressionable. It is modifiable.
2. The brain is divided. Each division came into existence at a different time in human evolutionary history.
3. Each division of the brain has specific capabilities for which it carries primary responsibility. If a particular division suffers damage, the capabilities of that division may be taken over by other divisions in the form of substitution or in the form of compensatory activity.
4. Each section of the brain is independent of the others. Each has its own source of energy. Each has its own internal organization, its own system of processing information and experiences, its own logic and goals. It has been suggested that each may have its own level of intelligence.
5. Every brain has a predesigned neural network. The design may be one that existed in persons of earlier generations (a hereditary throwback). It may be an example of nature's random experimenting, trial-and-error innovation by nature in its constant search for improvement. It may be a design consistent with nature's vast creativeness and pursuit of diversity.
6. Individuals differ in the brain designs with which they were born. Some are characterized by a complex network of neural fibers and many points of connection. Other brains have a simple network of neural fibers with few connections. Some brains have many centers of control through which stimuli are channeled; others, only one control center. Persons whom we describe as one-track-minded may be individuals with only one center of control available for information processing.
7. Brain designs can be altered. Neural fibers can atrophy if they are not used. At the same time, neural fibers can be developed through experience. We do not know yet whether the individual with only one center of control can develop a brain with more control centers. This possibility remains to be determined in laboratory testing of animals.
8. There is communication between brain hemispheres through the corpus callosum, a tube of neural fibers that connects the left and right sections.

9. The neural connections between the sections vary. For example, researchers are finding that there are few neural connections between the oldest part of the brain (the limbic section) and the second to the youngest part of the brain (the left hemisphere). Neural connections between the sections of the brain can be increased in number and performance improved through knowledge and experience. (This has been my clinical experience.)

10. Just as brains differ in design, they differ also in sectional centrality. Some people are limbic system dominated; others are right hemisphere dominated; still others are left hemisphere dominated.

11. The brain is the locus of the mind, the source of its roots and its nurturing. Like music, the mind goes far beyond its source. It has no boundaries. When in the course of our exploration of brain organization and design we refer to the brain-mind complex we will be touching on the ultimate paradox of the human estate: limitless potential emanating from three and one-half pounds of cells and neural fibers, encased in a nutshell.

12. The research findings remain to be further validated by empirical testing. The testing can be done with the use of well-established psychological testing procedures, for example the well-known Rorschach Inkblot Test.

The researcher Marilyn Fergusson postulates that the separateness of right and left hemispheres may vary in individuals. The cleavage between the two hemispheres may vary in size, thickness, and penetrability. In addition, interhemisphere activity may vary with mood and circumstance. Fergusson suggests that a new approach to brain research in this area is necessary in order to increase our understanding. One problem facing researchers, she points out, is their own deeply imbedded perceptions, which hinder their ability to approach familiar phenomena in a new way. According to Fergusson, nothing in current research indicates that what is stored in the right hemisphere can be erased. She suggests that perhaps one day children all over the world will offer their dreams at the breakfast table. The implication is that individuals will be intrigued with the creativeness and the imaginativeness of the right hemisphere, rather than frightened by hidden significance. [8]

The psychologist Janov, in the same vein, has suggested that human mentality may develop to the point that there is no unconscious. [9] Both hemispheres will be privy to the content of the other, and each will be available to the individual to pursue what he or she undertakes to do. The three sections of the brain functioning in harmony, each complementing the others, each contributing its own unique capability, under the direction, guidance, and control of the ego (the neural sheath), will make it possible for the individual to function at maximum capacity.

Variations in brain organization and brain design may well account for the facts that some people require more stimulation than others, that some are more flexible, and that some are more suggestible. Sectional dominance may account for interests, aptitudes, and talents. Sectional network design may account for inadequacies or disabilities in specific areas of functioning. For example, inadequate neural network design in the frontal lobe of the brain may account for difficulty in cognitive learning—the way one processes information and applies it to solve a problem.

Current technology should soon make available to us a topology of the brain, so that we will know the brain at least as well as we now know the body. We will be able to establish, test, and validate what now can only be hypothesized, namely:

  1. Problems in relationships come from the limbic system, as do problems associated with sex, out-of control behavior, and anger.
  2. Problems with concentration, practicality, time, sequence, success, fear, and anxiety have their locus in the right hemisphere.

3. Problems having to do with knowledge, logic, judgment, reason, and reality-perception have their locus in the left hemisphere.

4. Problems with values, priorities, and goals stem from the neural sheath that blankets the top of the left and right hemispheres.

With the problems localized, specific procedures for intervention will naturally evolve that are consistent with the function of the locale from which the difficulty stems.

CHAPTER 3

The Predesigned (Primitive) Brain: Its Operational Format

"Wouldn't it be a shame," Bob mused, "if nature had given the turtle a three-dimensional brain and the turtle chose to use only one dimension." This was no idle thought, no fantasy. Bob knew all too well what it was like to use only one part of the brain. For eight of his sixteen years he had been in a treatment institution, a prisoner of his right hemisphere. He lived in a fantasy world, struggling to survive in a real world. Early in life Bob had chosen to yield authority to the right hemisphere for control of his behavior. He remembers when his free will was lost and the right hemisphere took over. He remembers the remissions when he was better for a while. He remembers the recurrent psychotic episodes when reality receded and fantasy took over. His determination to keep right hemisphere activity under control was without qualification. It was difficult. The right hemisphere was powerful.

Brain researchers have found evidence that there are tens of thousands of points of entry to the neural network of the brain. [10] Stimuli at any point can trigger a chain reaction of change. In dealing with natural phenomena we do not have to wait for lightning to bring fire. Similarly, where psychological realities are concerned we can use knowledge, understanding, and insights to create the conditions necessary for human beings to prosper.

The Limbic Section: Life and Longing

The limbic section is undisputed in its evolutionary seniority. As we have seen, all the functions essential to living—breathing, hunger, circulation—are in the limbic section. The limbic area is also the site of emotional behavior—love, hate, anger, aggression.

Limbic Inadequacy and Power Abuse

The limbic section is primitive, simple, unsophisticated, and natural. It wants. It wants what it has had. Deeply imprinted in the limbic section is the womb experience. For nine months the embryo was nurtured and protected just because it "was." It didn't have to be anything special; it only had to "be." There was nothing in the womb experience that prepared the human psyche for the fact that once ejected from the womb these nurturing, protective conditions would never again exist. In this primal experience are the roots of the eternal human quest for the two-makes-one relationship; for the situation where wants and needs are satisfied without one's being aware that one has wants and needs; and for safety and security without end.

The limbic section's unawareness of reality—with what is possible, what is available—may reflect its lack of knowledge. It is important that we give the limbic section of the brain the benefit of the doubt. If it is behaving against the best interest of the individual, we must check whether it has the knowledge necessary to function differently. Lack of knowledge may come from the fact that the left hemisphere, the locus of knowledge and reality, is not adequately informed. Or it may be that the circuitry between the left hemisphere and the limbic section is nonexistent, inadequate, or nonfunctioning. Whatever the reason, the situation is correctable. The brain's constructive and reconstructive capacity is probably limitless if given the assistance it needs. We know little about the brain, and our techniques for assisting it are virtually nonexistent.

Seth was twelve. His behavior for the past two and one-half years had been intolerable. Now Mrs. K., his mother, was close to the breaking point. Her new marriage was in jeopardy. The other two children were experiencing problems in school and with their friends. Mrs. K. was certain that at the root of all these problems were the tensions Seth created in the home. She was considering placing him in a treatment institution. Mrs. K. had heard from a mutual friend about my new procedures based on brain research. She knew I did not usually work with children as young as Seth. She wondered if I would see him.

The time was not convenient. I was leaving for a media tour and a professional conference. But there was an urgency in Mrs. K.'s request. I agreed to see Seth for one interview, to be followed up when I returned. There was no guarantee that what I would do would help. Mrs. K. would have to watch closely Seth's reactions to the interview.

Seth, hair tousled and jeans stylishly faded, slouched in the chair nearest me. Did he know why his mother had wanted me to see him? He wasn't sure. I had the mother explain, then she left. Did Seth want to continue to live with the family? Seth indicated he had given that some thought because he knew the family had some question about that. Yes, he would like to live with the family. He thought they loved him. He certainly loved them.

As he considered the question of what made his family unhappy with him, Seth thought the main reason was the trouble he had with his brother. He had no idea why his brother was always angry with him. It never occurred to Seth that when he wanted to be with his brother his brother didn't want to be with him, and a fight always followed. Seth was not aware that another major problem was that he and his mother never agreed on anything and there was always an argument. The same thing happened at school on the baseball team. Many times Seth was on the verge of striking his teammates. He hadn't yet—but the intensity of his anger showed in his eyes. The acting out was an imminent possibility.

I explained to Seth the organization of the brain. He had studied physiology. He knew a little about the hemispheres. He had not heard about neural network design. He listened intently.

From what he and his mother had told me, it seemed to me, I said, that Seth had a problem in the limbic section of his brain. When there was a problem in the limbic section there were three things one had to examine: (1) did the limbic section know what it needed to know? (2) did the left hemisphere have the knowledge it needed to help the limbic section? (3) was there the necessary neural network for the knowledge to get through to the limbic section from the left hemisphere?

I gave Seth two assignments. During the two weeks that I was away he was to observe his brother. He was to keep a record of what he learned about his brother: specifically, the things his brother liked, the things he didn't like; the things that Seth did that annoyed his brother or made him angry; the things Seth did that he liked. Then Seth was to see whether what he learned got through to his limbic section and changed its reaction.

Two weeks later Seth came jauntily into the office. His hair was carefully combed. His head was high. He had the notebook with the notes he had made while I was away. He read them to me, proudly adding with obvious pleasure that he and his brother had had only one tiff while I was away. That was because Seth had misunderstood what his brother was doing. Also, Seth was doing better at school. Best of all, Seth had used his own money to buy a gallon of Pepsi to share with the family. A Cheshire-cat grin flooded his face as he told me proudly of this. For him, obviously, this had been a major achievement.

One interview—and psychotic-like behavior of two and one-half years duration under control; the beginnings of family cooperation and empathy. A miracle? Perhaps. But it was a miracle being repeated in case after case across a wide age spectrum and variety of disorders. How come? The brain organization-design frame of reference seems to do a number of things. It removes any suggestion of pathology. It localizes the problem. It specifies the problem and defines its boundaries so that the problem is approachable and manageable. It provides procedures for correcting the difficulty. It puts the individual in control. The person has a choice: to decide to do something about the problem or to leave it as is. The crucial fact that Seth had to grapple with was that if he remained "as is" he very likely could not remain with his family. His wish to remain with them provided powerful motivation to do whatever was in his power to correct what was placing his security in jeopardy.

There are times when the limbic section pulls rank. As the seat of life-sustaining systems the limbic section is supreme. There are times when it takes an autocratic stance, giving priority to its self-interest rather than to the interests of the personality as a whole.

Nan was determined. She was going to be a physician. Her experience as an undergraduate had been difficult. While she was extremely bright, there were things that her brain with its predesigned pattern was simply unable to do. Through a stroke of luck Nan learned of some new procedures to correct her problem. The procedures worked. Learning now was not only exciting. It was fun, and the level of her achievement astounded her professors.

Another problem surfaced. Every time she sat down to write the paper for which she had done extensive research, she became ravenously hungry or painfully tired. Neither reaction had reality. She had had adequate meals and more than adequate sleep.

Apparently, the limbic section was feeling at risk, its domain in jeopardy. It was making a last ditch stand to sabotage left hemisphere activity. In that last ditch stand it was employing, illegitimately, power that lay within its organic jurisdiction, the power over energy flow (breathing and respiration expressed in fatigue) and hunger.

Nan had had many occasions over the years to exert left hemisphere control over the limbic section of her brain. Depression no longer plagued her. She no longer looked for the two-makes-one relationship. She knew her needs and wants had to be acknowledged and expressed if they were to be satisfied. Nan had the knowledge she needed to have where the demands of advanced study were concerned. She was clear as to her values, priorities, and goals. She was a committed, dedicated student. What the limbic section had to be assured of was that its power and authority would be recognized, but within the framework of left hemisphere needs and ego-determined goals. Instinct, reflex, or habit would not dominate in the management of Nan's life. It was a painstaking task. The limbic section was not easily convinced.

The process was much like that used by nursery schools: short periods of study followed by short periods of rest or exercise or snacks. The periods of study were lengthened and the breaks shortened as the limbic system would tolerate this program. The conversation between the left hemisphere and the limbic section was frequent, persistent, and firm. The limbic section would have its rightful place in the way Nan lived her life. It would not rule. The battle—and it was a battle—has been won. A more delighted, excited young woman would be difficult to find in this ever-expanding global society of ours.

Clinicians know that anger can spawn asthma because it can interfere with breathing. Anger can cause colitis because it can interfere with digestion. Fear, real or imagined, can bring on heart palpitations and affect circulation. In other words, the limbic section can use its emotional repertoire to interfere with the operational systems of the total human organism. This is a misuse of its assigned power and jurisdiction.

The autonomic systems—breathing, circulation, digestion—are to the human body what the sun, the moon, and the stars are to the universe. They belong to the whole. They were intended to work in harmony to the best interest of the whole. The limbic section, when it expresses its anger or fear in biological terms, is overstepping its jurisdiction. It is diverting to its self-interest energy and power to which other parts of the brain-mind complex have at least equal claim. Such misuse of jurisdiction and energy diversion must be stopped in the interest of the individual's physical and mental health.

Issues of jurisdiction and rights are matched in urgency with the vast question of relationships which fall within the limbic authority, stemming primarily from the womb experience and the expectations that have derived from it. There seems to be deeply embedded in our brain cells of the limbic section the memory of the womb experience and the hope coupled with the wish that that "utopia" would at some time again be our reality. Life experience, knowledge, and reason seem to have no effect upon that hope and wish.

If we stop to think about it, we know that the limbic section has among its many capabilities the capacity to change. We know, for example, that its elementary emotions of love, hate, anger, passion, and aggression can be developed into the higher reaches of emotion: empathy, sympathy, compassion, fairness, and justice. We know that the limbic section can yield its self-centeredness to the requirements of social living. We may expect that if the realities of relationships are made clear, the limbic section could shed its unrealistic wishes and devote its energies to making the most of what is possible, making the most of the best of reality.

Knowledge Checklist: The Limbic Section

The limbic section by virtue of its evolutionary seniority may be considered the repository of primary characteristics, essential to the organism's well-being. We may assume that nature in usual fashion has invested each characteristic with the capability of change, for change is intrinsic to nature, and capability for change is essential for survival.

Sensation, feeling, and experiencing are the specific, unique domain of the limbic section. To subject sensation, feeling, and experiencing to conscious examination involves a specific process. The process does not come naturally—it must be designed and practiced. One must expect resistance. In most instances the enterprise will be undertaken only if there is no choice. The whole human system, as all other phenomena of nature, prefers the status quo, the pattern that requires the least expenditure of energy. That is the law of nature that probably transcends all others. Inertia is our preference if there is a choice.

It is little wonder that we have difficulty with relationships in this volatile world. Some realities specific to the human estate have been camouflaged in the past by the demands of survival. People in past generations have been content with the "pursuit of happiness" as a goal. Today, we want happiness not as a distant probability but as something here and now that we can touch and feel. Our expectations are as astronomical as the federal budget. The federal budget is incomprehensible but real. While expectations may be specific, they are elusive. As one theorist put it: "We don't know what we want, but we won't stop until we get it."

It is best if we know what we want. It is essential that we know if what we want is available. To want what is not available is to live a life of frustration, wasting energy on unrealistic anger. Human relationships stand out as a glaring example of an area in which we hold unrealistic expectations.

Misled as we have been by the womb experience, we do not recognize certain indisputable realities:

Two people do not make one.

Love is not a birthright. It carries no warranty or lifetime guarantee. In most human relationships to be loved one must be lovable.

Passion may be magnetic, but like a bolt of lightning it can be spent in a flash. There is in it no guarantee of permanence.

All individuals are separate and distinct, with their own genetic history and their own pattern of perceptions, reactions, and ways of processing information.

All individuals are by nature autonomous, not subject to the will and whims of others unless they desire to be. Their will is distinctly their own. They have choices which they may engage or not. That is their prerogative, as endowed by nature.

Given these realities what right does one have to be angry, to hate, to act out against others? All too often anger is a distortion of hurt. How much easier it is to lash out against an offending party than to nurse the psychological injury the individual may have inflicted, whether knowingly or unknowingly. Realistically, it is better to nurse the hurt so that it heals than to indulge anger. Anger has no healing properties, and it is probably the most draining and debilitating of human emotions.

If as we deal with our particular modes of sensation, feeling, and experiencing we are aware of our expectations and can check them out for validity, appropriateness, and availability, we can spare ourselves the anger of hurt, the hurt of anger. And one need never run the risk of primitive acting out. A vast reservoir of energy is freed for use, and new horizons open up.

Four interviews. We had examined how the three sections of Samantha's brain had been working to have brought Samantha to the point of suicide. The only thing that had kept her alive was her feeling for her two children. At nine and six years of age, they could never understand why she would have chosen to leave them.

Her parents, relatives, and friends scolded her. She had so much. She should be grateful. What if Bob was a philanderer? He supported the family not only adequately but very comfortably. It seemed to be his pleasure to do so. He was proud of their home, with its swimming pool and tennis court. It didn't matter to Bob that he was never home enough to enjoy any of it. Providing it was all that he required. Nor could he understand Samantha's unhappiness. All she wanted was everything—not only his earnings but his attention and involvement in her life. These she could not have. Bob did not have them to give.

The realities were clear. Samantha could have her wants and needs satisfied, perhaps even before she knew she had those wants and needs. She could have safety and security and comfort. These were well within Bob's ability to provide. What she could not have was the two-makes-one relationship. Bob was not available. He wasn't interested. He couldn't be.

The fact that in this marriage Samantha could not have the two-makes-one relationship for which she desperately longed posed a serious problem. Could she make her peace with what she could have in her marriage? Samantha was clear—she could not. It was not enough to warrant the effort of living. Was Samantha enough of a person in her own right that she could go it alone or until she could find someone who would provide the linkage she required? She did not know. It seemed to her that in spite of her many skills and accomplishments (there had been many in her thirty-eight years) she had never had confidence in herself. She could remember only the things she hadn't done well or that she thought she should have done better. She could think only of her family's impatience with her. They seemed to focus on what she was not doing, not on what she was doing and had done. What they thought of her was overwhelmingly important.

The limbic section was the locus of Samantha's problems. What were the realities—in terms of relationships, her capabilities, and the things she wanted for herself? Samantha took hold quickly. She was going to stop behaving like a child, expecting a return to the womb. She was going to take responsibility for assessing her own activities and directing her energies into channels that would give her a good feeling about herself. She would find a job that provided challenge. She might even go back to school and get her master's degree in her chosen field.

Four interviews. A metamorphosis in appearance—Samantha looked ten years younger—and in attitude—there was a buoyancy about her that bespoke enthusiasm, excitement, and optimism. Samantha was delighted, and grateful for what we had done together. Never in her life had she slept so well or had so much energy. Never had she enjoyed reading so much or the hours that were completely her own. She was seeing friends and relatives, but only those who could add something positive to her life. It was amazing how her family was responding. They were changing. They were impressed and delighted with the change they felt in her. We had accomplished more than she dreamed possible. She did not need to see me again.

Apparently, Samantha's left hemisphere was equipped with the necessary knowledge, and her limbic section had the required skills for selfhood. The speed with which the procedure worked (and this is not unusual) indicates that the neural connections were there to be used. Had there been a blockage? What had been amiss that Samantha had not herself been able to make the changes that her marriage required? We do not know. We can conjecture.

Did Samantha buy the "bill of goods" our society has been selling: "You're nobody till somebody loves you"?

Did she really believe that "Love is all there is; Love will see you through in the end"?

Was she protesting the responsibility that comes with adulthood out of fear or lack of confidence in her judgment? If so, what was the fear? Why the lack of confidence?

What was clear was that the voice of the limbic section prevailed: "I want." The voice of the left hemisphere—"I want the most of the best that I can have"—was virtually silent. Caught in the vacuum between the two was Samantha's fantastically rich right hemisphere—rich in dreams, well equipped with wings. We may expect that the future will find Samantha flying free. But her feet will be firmly on the ground, guided by her values, priorities, and goals and by whatever reality she chooses for herself.

For Martha, limbic "wanting" was not so easily divested of its urgency.

Martha was in her early sixties. For the past four years, her marriage of thirty-six years had been a marriage in name only. Randall had moved out early one fall morning. Nothing unusual had happened, just the familiar bickering that had characterized their marriage and the growing-up years of their four children. The children were on their own: the oldest by his own choice, the other three at the insistence of their parents. Randall and Martha had agreed: parenthood was an "episode" that had an ending where responsibility was concerned. Dependency without end neither of them could tolerate.

For the first months after Randall moved out he "played the field." Then he settled in with Erma. He was going to plays and concerts with her, interests he never shared with Martha. Randall has not asked for a divorce. Martha is under the impression that he really doesn't want one. To be free would mean for him a second marriage, and he seems not to want that. Other things also kept Martha confused. When matters went badly for her financially Randall increased his monthly payment to her. Recently, he had helped her buy a car. At the same time, he adamantly refused to spend any time with her socially. He just wasn't interested.

In spite of the fact that Martha's memories of her marriage are unhappy, she is inconsolable. She loves Randall. She is determined to hold him to his marriage vow "till death do us part."

There is a problem. Martha had to quit her job as a dental technician because she was emotionally distraught. She felt on the verge of a nervous breakdown. And she was frightened by her increasingly frequent thoughts of suicide.

Just in the last few months her financial situation has changed. She inherited some money, not a great deal, but enough to allow her to manage independently. She has begun to think of a divorce. She is able to identify three things that a divorce would do for her: (1) it would return her self-respect; (2) it would leave her free to date, which she could not do while she was married; and (3) she could attend singles groups and extend the range of her friendships. Martha was able also to review her many interests, talents, and capabilities—and they were many. There was even a moment when her eyes sparkled and her complexion took on a new glow as she considered what she might do with her life if she shed the anger, the frustration, and the bitterness engendered by Randall.

Then her excitement faded. She wouldn't know how or where to begin. What she really wanted to do was file an alienation suit against Erma, not for damages but to force her husband to come back.

We had come full circle. We had examined the realities. We had explored the options and the cost each carried, psychologically, socially, and economically. The limbic section had heard none of it. It "wanted," no matter what. It had no concern with whether what it wanted was available.

Martha had had exposure to psychology when she studied to be a dental technician. She had had some psychotherapy with a person whose basic theories seemed much like mine. She had recently heard of another school of thought and would explore that before she made any firm decision as to how to proceed.

What accounted for the difference between Samantha's and Martha's responses to the same theory? Was it age? Samantha was in her thirties; Martha, in her sixties. The women were equally bright and accomplished, albeit in different fields, but in fields requiring equivalent capacities.

Each had known another therapist. Each was conversant with theories of psychology. Samantha heard and processed what went on in the first interview and was able to act on it immediately. Apparently, the neural connection between her left hemisphere and limbic section was well developed and open. The limbic section heard, understood, and acted upon its new knowledge without delay. Martha heard and understood. At moments she was intrigued and excited. But the conclusion was that we ended where we started. Had Martha returned for another interview, one of the first steps would have been to determine whether there is a neural connection between her left hemisphere and the limbic section. Possibly one exists, but it may be open only to certain data and closed to others.

Questions of this nature and scope remain unanswered. We need more definitive information concerning how the brain functions. We need to know more about the neural network: where it may be inadequate to the task at hand; where there may be a short circuiting of neural fibers or inadequate connecting links. All of these areas may be checked through verbal exploration. Construction, reconstruction, and the development of connecting links can all be achieved without either chemical or electrical intervention. Ideas can be the catalyst, the converter, the conveyor, and even the disassembler where connections are faulty or disruptive.

The limbic section no doubt has in its memory recollections of the time when it was in sole control of the human organism. It may recall with some nostalgia that two million-year period when it, together with the right hemisphere, ruled the psychological domain of the human organism. Preprogrammed by nature, these two sections of the brain were compatible. They complemented each other, and each in its own way added to the life experience of the human organism. Why nature created the left hemisphere is a valid question. Why the new development was so different, and why it had the right to make demands on its senior counterparts, are legitimate concerns. Nature no doubt had its reasons.

The Right Hemisphere: Wings and Worries

The right hemisphere can be likened to a vast, varied tract of land, with mountains and valleys, lakes and deserts, underground caverns, turbulent rivers, and waterfalls. Like the earth with its relics and fossils of the Stone Age and the Ice Age, in the right hemisphere is the archaeological record of the brain. In it one can find remnants of the mandates of ancient gods; the instructions and prohibitions of ancestors, parents, and mentors; the fantasies, wishes, and fears of the child's inexperienced mind. The archaeological remnants in the earth, according to our current perceptions, do not provide us with current power. This is not true of the archaeological remnants of the mind. There the residuals of the past harbor energy and exert power.

The right hemisphere, like the limbic section, is unencumbered by reality or time. It functions as though it were a world complete unto itself, omniscient and omnipotent. It relies on the what-has-beens (the laws of inertia, gravity, and conservation). In its imaginativeness and its propensity for fancy it draws on the law of magnetism. All of this, however, is undertaken and managed according to the organization and design programmed by nature. Being of the same generation as the limbic section in evolutionary time, the right hemisphere often teams up with the limbic section, in collusion against the left hemisphere where either or both feel themselves in jeopardy.

Sue had finally made it. For the first time in her thirty-five years her brilliance was showing through. Her fellow students and the professors were impressed and spurred her on. Sue had always been a dreamer of bold dreams. These characteristics, coupled with her enthusiasm and her charisma, made her a compelling figure. But somewhere she fell short. Her actual accomplishments were marginal. The traditional therapeutic route of examining history, feelings, attitudes, and goals had been clarifying and comforting but had not relieved the problems Sue had always had in a learning situation.

Recent brain research findings offered new avenues of approach. There was no question: Sue was right hemisphere dominated. She thought in global terms. She saw clearly the whole but not the parts. Her dreams were vividly colorful, action-packed. She loved the wide-open spaces.

By comparison her left hemisphere was underdeveloped. It could not detect the difference between a "generalization" and a "specific." It did not know what was "description" and what was a "rule." It did not know how to break a problem into its component parts, or which step should precede which.

A new neural network had to be developed. There were three specific steps. They had to be practiced, much as one practices the scales if one wants to play the piano. The procedures worked. A new neural network was developed.

Studying, learning, and writing had finally become fun. In fact, they became the focus of Sue's life, and she loved every minute of it. But there was a problem.

Sue would go to bed feeling healthy exhaustion. While sleep came easily and readily, night after night it was charged with vivid, catastrophic dreams. The invaders were coming. Unless she did something to stop them, they would destroy her entire family and herself. Or there would be a fire, and only through unusual ingenuity could she avoid being trapped. The horrors were persistent and frighteningly explicit. Her escape possibilities became narrower. Sue awakened exhausted and shaken. She knew what she had to do. She had to remind her right hemisphere that it had a right to be worried or frightened if it wanted to be. But it did not have the right to interfere with the activities of the left hemisphere through its unrealistic worries and fears. There was no real reason why the right hemisphere should be worried or afraid. Sue was an adult.

She knew what was right and what was wrong. She knew what was reality and what was fantasy. She cared. She knew and respected the rights of others. Never would she do anything intentionally that would be hurtful or harmful to anyone.

Sue was quite aware of her abilities and limitations. In whatever she undertook to do, she would be guided by knowledge, logic, and reason in accordance with her values, priorities, and goals. The right hemisphere did not have to worry that its domain would be destroyed. In the way Sue would design her life, it would have a unique and rightful place.

Only occasionally, now, do the nightmares return. For the most part, Sue's dreams are pleasant—even playful—reflecting the achievements and the gratifications of the day just passed.

Vast wealth lies in the right hemisphere. Like diamonds embedded in coal and pearls hidden in oysters, the riches of the right hemisphere may be hidden from view. This wealth may have to be chiseled out of the rock in which it crystallized. Likewise in human beings, there may be hidden resources. However, over the past two hundred years we have not developed procedures for digging out these latent gems. Society needed round pegs to fit round holes and square pegs to fit square holes. And we proceeded to produce them. In today's electronic world the requirements will be different. But with the sophisticated technology we now have, the functioning of the human brain should be manifest in all of its possibilities. The human organism will not for long remain an untapped reality.

CHAPTER 4

The Postprimitive Brain: Line of Authority

The Left Hemisphere: "Let's Look at the Facts"

There was no territorial invasion of other brain areas when the left hemisphere came into being. The brain doubled in size by evolutionary fiat. But the left hemisphere signaled a change of major significance in brain functioning. The left hemisphere is different in several ways. For example, it asks questions; it compares; it reflects; it exercises logic; it makes judgments. This half of the brain is keenly aware of objective reality and has a real sense of time and of sequence. As an addition to the brain complex, the left hemisphere seems strange—even foreign. If the older sections of the brain have a consciousness, they may well have wondered what nature was up to in introducing this new portion. And well they may have wondered. For nature in creating the left hemisphere registered that in its judgment instinct, reflex, habit—the capabilities of reptiles, birds, and fish—were no longer suffi-cient to ensure survival of the human species. In characteristic fashion, nature created the equipment necessary for species survival. The left hemisphere by its very existence came with a mandate—to introduce into the brain complex the capacities for knowledge, logic, reason, judgment, reality, and a sense of time.

We do not know whether the older sections of the brain have a consciousness of nature and its indisputable authority. We do know from experience that neither the limbic section nor the right hemisphere has taken kindly to the presence of the left hemisphere. These older sections have resisted the demands that the left hemisphere has placed upon them in its effort to fulfill the mandate that came with its creation.

Demands: Left Hemisphere on Limbic Section

Until the left hemisphere came into being the limbic section was sufficient unto itself. It was preprogrammed by nature while still in its embryonic state. It responded according to a preset pattern. A particular stimulus elicited a specific response. The limbic section did not have to make choices. It could do what came naturally, with the least expenditure of effort and energy. The limbic section in its natural state did not concern itself with knowledge or rights or limits or reality. Its wants were simple and primary. Satisfaction was dictated by instinct, reflex, and habit.

But with the evolution of the left hemisphere, the limbic section found itself face to face with new and different issues, issues with which it was unequipped to deal. In its natural state the limbic section knew only what was deeply imbedded in its brain cells. It experienced. It reacted. It felt. It did not think. Self-centered and self-contained, functioning on command of natural forces, the limbic system had no capacity for objective knowledge, logic, or judgment. It knew no reality outside itself. The left hemisphere, with its focus on knowledge, logic, reason, and judgment, and its concern with reality, was not only a stranger to the limbic section. The left hemisphere was a foreigner, with a different way of perceiving, processing, and monitoring life experiences.

The left hemisphere expected the limbic section to recognize that it was not the center of the universe but that it was a part of a unit. It was unique, special. It was not alone, absolute. It had rights, but its rights were limited by the rights of others. It had authority, but it had to take into account the authority of others. And because of its evolutionary seniority, it had great power. That power, if the individual was to prosper, would have to be used in the best interest of the whole.

The left hemisphere expected that the emotional reservoir over which the limbic section had primary jurisdiction would be refined and distilled into the higher-level states of sensitivity, sympathy, empathy, and compassion. And that energy would be developed for commitment and dedication as activities in other sections of the brain complex required.

The left hemisphere looked to the limbic section for rootedness, for the sense of belonging. It looked to the limbic section for relatedness—the enrichment that comes with having people in one's life; for feelings that add depth, color, and vitality to experiencing. What the limbic system had available to contribute to the whole was unique and special. No other section of the brain was equipped with its capabilities. The domain of the limbic section was secure, inviolate. Its autonomy, however, was not without limits. Its power could not be used indiscriminately. Both its autonomy and its power would be subject to control in deference to the welfare of the organism as a whole, so that the individual would live in health and with the opportunity for maximum fulfillment.

Our world offers dramatic evidence that the limbic system has not yielded to the expectations of the left hemisphere. Except in the areas of science and technology, the left hemisphere has made few inroads in effecting change. Our society has given center stage to feelings and passion. Knowledge is viewed with suspicion. Is it the relative youth of the left hemisphere that has spawned this lack of confidence? Or has it stemmed from the fact that it is much easier to function according to instinct, reflex, and habit as preprogrammed by nature?

We know now from experience that the limbic section will not easily yield its power. It will relinquish its influence only if it must. It will yield only if the left hemisphere exerts sufficient force to keep limbic power and influence under control.

Demands: Left Hemisphere on Right Hemisphere

The demands the left hemisphere made of the right hemisphere were less in both quality and quantity than those it made on the limbic system. Essentially, all the left hemisphere required of the right hemisphere was that it not interfere with left hemisphere functioning. The right hemisphere could continue to enjoy imagination, fantasy, rhythm, space. It could continue to be indifferent to time and reality as long as its activities complemented or supplemented the activities of the left hemisphere. The right hemisphere provides dreams and wings. It brings into play the third basic law of nature: the law of magnetism. The left hemisphere would not need to call upon the mandates of ancient gods or the taboos of the past. It would be developing rules for human behavior based on knowledge as it developed and as dictated by logic, reason, and judgment. It had as its ally the neural sheath, some 3,000 to 5,000 years old, with its focus on values, priorities, and goals; with its vision of humanity governed by honesty, integrity, compassion, and justice. It was not the dream world of the right hemisphere in its expansive moments that the left hemisphere aimed to achieve. It was a world in which the highest dreams based on the most highly valued human capabilities could be realized.

When one views the achievements of humankind over the past 5,000 years, especially those of the past 500 years, one must be impressed. We have progressed from the Stone Age to the Space Age. We have harnessed the airwaves, making possible instant intercontinental communication. We have replaced kidneys and hearts in the human body. We are on the verge of implanting cameras so that those without vision can see. Today's world abounds with the marvels of science and technology. In comparison, our achievements in the human dimension are meager indeed. In the area of emotions and human relationships, we are still functioning primarily by instinct, reflex, and habit. Our rejection of difference is appalling, as exemplified by the prejudices we have against those who are different from ourselves in terms of race, culture, or religion. Our resistance to change is intense (limbic section). Our development of human potential, for example, imagination, whose source is the right hemisphere, has been minimal except as it has been commandeered by the left hemisphere.

Maybe our minimal achievement can be ascribed to the resistance of the limbic section and the right hemisphere to being a part of a larger synchronized whole. Maybe, however, the source of the problem is an inadequacy in neural connections: between the left hemisphere and the limbic where emotions and human relations are in question; and between the left hemisphere and the right hemisphere where human potential is under consideration.

Where knowledge, logic, reason, reality, and time do not register appropriately in human behavior, let's look to the neural connections. Are they adequate for knowledge to be channeled from the left hemisphere to the limbic section so that logic, reason, and judgment can operate? Where human behavior is faulty in terms of time, space, and reality, let's make sure the neural connections between the left and right hemispheres are adequate to keep the boundaries clear. In both instances, adequate knowledge is paramount in order for the left hemisphere to exercise the authority and set the boundaries and controls necessary for it to carry out nature's mandate.

The Neural Sheath: The Executive Branch

Place a postage stamp at the very tip of the Empire State Building. This example barely illustrates the age of the neural sheath, the newest section of the brain, in terms of the rest. We are talking about 3,000 to 5,000 years as compared with 300,000 to 3 million years—an infinitesimal time span indeed.

What is equally striking is that in its very brief history this section of the brain has witnessed, perhaps spurred, tremendous achievements. In science and technology achievements in the last 500 years have surpassed those in any other period of human history as far as we know. It is estimated that the first catastrophic change in human history, the move from primitive to civilized society, took place some 5,000 years ago. This dating coincides with the outer estimate of the time the neural sheath came into being. At approximately the same time, the Israelites during their desert wanderings developed the first moral code, a document of 613 items that were distilled in the ten commandments.

Apparently, something of tremendous significance and potency came into being with the neural sheath. Contemporary brain researchers are finding evidence suggesting that the neural sheath is the area of the brain in which is housed consciousness, or awareness of self; awareness of others; and the capacity to make choices, to be responsible. From the capacity to make choices there developed a need for guidelines to direct choice and to form judgments. Adjuncts to consciousness are values, priorities, and goals—that is, social awareness—hence the moral code.

The neural sheath as the executive branch of the brain complex carries tremendous responsibility. It must decide where the neural impulses go. Do they belong within the domain of the limbic section, the right hemisphere, or the left hemisphere? It must make decisions pertaining to content, intent, and goal.

Where values, priorities, and goals are not firmly defined, the executive branch of the brain has difficulty directing behavior. The result is inconsistency, vacillation, confusion. The most dramatic example is found in individuals who repeatedly achieve success and for no apparent reason scuttle it. Their lives take on the up-and-down pattern of the yo-yo, or the back-and-forth motion of the teeter-totter—back and forth from success to failure and back again.

The Executive "I": The Final Authority

Two inches behind the eye in the very center of the brain (the pineal gland), says the biologist Colin Blakemore, is the "me-ness of me," the part of the personality that earlier theorists like Aristotle called the "soul." The "me-ness of me," or the "me-myself-I," is that subtle, indefinable quality that distinguishes one individual from another. It is the thread that runs through an individual's perceptions, attitudes, feelings, reactions, and actions that reflect an internal consistency, even if that "consistency" is in essence "inconsistency," an up-and-downness, an in-and-outness. It is the core, much like the core of an apple or the pit of a plum. In the human personality that "me-ness of me" is the final authority. Like the authority of the President of the United States, it may be final but it is not absolute.

A Revolt

There is evidence that the authority of the "me" can be overridden by the different parts of the brain, much as the President's authority can be overridden by Congress. Ingrid is a graphic case in point.

> Ingrid was in a postgraduate university program. She had volunteered for an honor's program project. Some unique aspects of Ingrid's educational background and experience made her particularly suited to the project in question. Her professor was delighted that she would undertake it. He thought it might add significantly to the experience she and the other students were engaged in. Ingrid had a year to work on it. That seemed plenty of time.
>
> Six months had gone by. Occasionally—very occasionally—a fleeting reminder of the project would flash through her mind, much like a comet streaks across the sky and disappears. She had done some of the necessary research. She had written an introduction and a tentative outline. She had thought about what might go into the first chapter. That was all. Her professor had stopped in the hall one day and asked her quite casually how the project was coming along. She answered him casually, reassuringly. Suddenly she found herself not at all casual. Not at all assured. Her program had been very demanding. She had not been wasting time. A year was a long time. She certainly should have no problem fulfilling her commitment. The executive "I" was reassuring the left hemisphere. There was no problem.

But maybe this was the time for Ingrid to get back to work on the project instead of taking on the chairmanship of a continuing education program in which she was interested.

Ingrid was very well acquainted with her right hemisphere and its well developed "All I want is everything" pattern. She always has to be on the alert for the tendency of her brain/mind system to overextend, to overdraw its intellectual bank account.

Her decision was firm. She would turn down the chairmanship. She would begin on her project the next day. In preparation she went to bed early. She had an amazingly restful sleep and awakened full of energy, eager to get started.

The first hour went well. She reviewed the research material she had gathered. She was surprised to find how much she had already written. It held up well even with the passage of time. She reviewed the abstract of her project and her outline.

Suddenly there was a change. Her eyelids became heavy. She was exhausted. There was a gnawing in the pit of her stomach as though she hadn't eaten for days. She recognized the symptoms. They were familiar. In fact, she had struggled with them all of her learning life. They were her psyche in protest. The brain/mind complex was being overtaken, overrun by the right hemisphere empowered by her three-year-old fantasy of omnipotence, omniscience: "I know all there is to know, I can do whatever anyone else can do." Ingrid's logical mind (the left hemisphere) knew better. It knew that it didn't know all there was to know. It knew that it couldn't do whatever anyone else could do. There was certainly ample evidence of that everywhere. But Ingrid's right hemisphere had not given up the fantasy. It had indulged Ingrid's left hemisphere in that it had allowed it to learn, but only under massive protest. The situation resembled that of the eager child and the recalcitrant mother:

> Mother, mother may I go to swim?
> Yes, my darling daughter.
> Hang your clothes on a hickory limb
> But don't go near the water.

The right hemisphere is not the mother of the left hemisphere. It may think it could be, even that it should be. But it isn't. The left hemisphere is a creation of nature. It has at least an equal right to "be" as the right hemisphere. We must consider the possibility that being among nature's most recent creations it may in fact be of superior caliber to nature's earlier inventions. It is very possible that in the 2½ to 3 million years between the origin of the limbic section-right hemisphere and the left hemisphere nature may have learned. It may have discovered through experience where its original inventions were lacking and set about to correct the lacks.

At any rate, nothing Ingrid did to bring right hemisphere interference under control worked—a nap, a snack, a long walk through the woods. Ingrid was angry. The right hemisphere did not have the right to immobilize the left hemisphere. It did not have a right to draw on the life-sustaining autonomic systems—breathing, respiration, appetite—located in the biological domain of its ally, the limbic section, to aid it in its sabotage. It may not have the "right," but it had the power. Whether right or not, it was using that power. A revolt within the psychic system was in full swing. Ingrid was exhausted. She, the executive "I," had lost. A whole day had gone by. She had accomplished nothing.

Panic took hold. Was she never going to be able to do what she wanted to do? Was that infantile part of her always going to win in spite of all she knew? Was learning, writing, and taking responsibility always going to be attended by such psychological torture? If so, was it worth it? Was life worth it? There was nothing else Ingrid wanted to do more than what she was doing now—studying, learning, experiencing, venturing new academic and experiential challenges. She was desperate.

Desperation was not new. It was as much a part of her life as her *joie de vivre*, her joy of living. She knew from experience that always she mastered the desperation and went on to high achievement. What she had not realized was that repeatedly her psyche had protested vehemently at any semblance of a "must." Tell it that it "must" and instinctively, adamantly, it asserted "I won't." This was as consistent and firmly set a pattern as the desperation and the *joie de vivre*.

With thirty-five years of learning experience to her credit Ingrid still did not "know" her brain. She wanted autocratic control. She could not have it. Her brain was a democracy. Each part insisted on autonomy and rights. It would not tolerate a dictatorship no matter how well intentioned or how lofty its intent.

Ingrid was at a crossroads. If she was to survive (literally), she had to devise a strategy for bringing the three sections of her brain into harmony under the direction of the neural sheath values, priorities, goals. Her executive "I" had to concede it could not succeed by executive order.

Organizational Realities

Decision-making is the task assigned by nature to the executive "I" (the pineal gland has been found to emit impulses that activate the nervous system). [11] Where, as with Ingrid, the sections of the brain do not function as a team under the direction of the neural sheath and at the request of the executive "I," some simple preliminary strategies may be necessary. We have ample evidence from life in general that if you want something *not* to get done, tell the person he or she "must." Evidence of this reaction is found in newborns. Apparently it comes with the genes, a part of the preprogramming by nature. The most productive approach is enticement: "wouldn't it be nice if. . . ." We come into the world highly responsive to stimulation and to challenges, provided they are within the range of our comprehension and our abilities. A next step would be to consider what the plan involves in terms of time, energy, and involvement. What are its demands on each section of the brain: time and study (left hemisphere); imagination, creativeness (right hemisphere); energy, commitment, tolerance of frustration (limbic section). A meeting of the brain/mind sections would be in order to determine willingness, readiness, and ability to undertake what the executive "I" would like to do.

If agreement and cooperation prove not to be possible, the executive "I" must be placed under scrutiny. Has it overstepped the boundaries of itself? Is it reaching beyond the outer limits of its organic capabilities? Is the relationship between the sections of the brain unclear, unstable? Can the energies that are being used to sabotage be redirected in the interest of the whole? Has the executive "I" achieved the level of maturity necessary for it to be the final authority in a team enterprise?

Is it fully aware of the realities, internal and external?

Does it have confidence in its judgment?

Is it firm in its authenticity—can it establish its own standards of performance and concern itself only with the opinions of those it respects?

Is it vigilant of the risks and assured of ways to deal with them?

The executive "I" when fully developed is a master of versatility. Its repertoire of options is vast. If one goal proves unattainable, there are others. If one course is blocked, it finds or establishes others. The executive "I" may find itself momentarily stymied, in a quandary or immobilized. But only momentarily, for it knows well the principle of emergence, the on-the-move, in-process character of nature's pattern.

CHAPTER 5

Orchestration: The Brain in Concert

Consider the three sections of the brain (limbic, right hemisphere, left hemisphere) under the direction of the conductor (the neural sheath), with the producer (the me-myself-I) in the wings overseeing the production and determining its basic theme, mood, and eventual coherence.

The left hemisphere with its knowledge, reason, logic, and judgment, and with its commitment to reality and time, looks to the senior partners to contribute to the whole from their specific talents. Exclusive to the limbic section are:

The basic emotions—love, hate, anger, passion, aggression—and their advanced manifestation—sensitivity, sympathy, empathy, and compassion, together with the capacity for dedication and commitment.

The importance of relationships.

The dynamic interplay of the three basic laws of nature: gravity or inertia, conservation, and magnetism.

To the right hemisphere the left hemisphere looks for:

The flights of fancy (imagination).

Hopes and dreams.

The pulling into a cohesive whole the bits and pieces that accumulate at random.

Rhythm in even flow and turbulence—the color, excitement of variety, adventure.

Unencumbered by concerns of reality and time, the right hemisphere has at its command the ancestral past, the present, and through its flights of fancy projections of the future. What's more, it can, if it chooses, conjure up out of the varied, dissimilar parts a whole. It doesn't have to make sense. As far as we know there are no rules to which the right hemisphere adheres. It is its own designer and critic. In its versatility and exuberance it is inviting, seductive. In its self-view everything is at its command, and everything is dictated by what it wants and expects.

To bring the right hemisphere under control one needs only to set the limits of its activities. One does not have to educate. As a matter of fact, researchers are finding evidence to confirm what clinicians have known for years. What is lodged in the right hemisphere seems to be not subject to change. How and why the content was selected for storage we do not know. How and to what end it became so deeply imbedded we seem unable to determine with our current knowledge of brain functioning and our current skills.

The situation seems to be quite different with the limbic section. The limbic section seems to be educable. Given the necessary knowledge, being advised of realities—what is possible, what is impossible—it seems to be able to alter its reactions and its expectations. That the limbic section so often has failed to keep up with changing realities may be the fault of the brain's neural network. Researchers are finding that in most individuals the neural connections between the limbic section and the left hemisphere are sparse or nonexistent. In other words, there has been no channel for information to flow from the left hemisphere to the limbic section. The limbic section therefore does not know about reality or time or substantive knowledge or the exercise of reason and logic. Its operations and the scope of them are impressive and have been entirely via the neural network predesigned by nature. The limbic section contains a vast store of knowledge and wisdom, but it is inherited, instinctive knowledge and wisdom that came with the genes and experience. It is knowledge and wisdom that has not been subject to conscious, systematic examination and validation. There is massive resistance to this in fact. Intuitively the limbic section seems to know that once intuitive knowledge and wisdom are subjected to conscious examination, security in it is lost. There is no one who knows as surely what he or she knows than the one who has never studied or learned.

Procedures for Orchestration

With the executive producer committed to left hemisphere control under the direction of the neural sheath, the procedures are simple. They are simpler for the right hemisphere than for the limbic section. To keep the right hemisphere under control, the left hemisphere needs only three steps. It must be alert to right hemisphere interference, that is, when the right hemisphere:

> **1.** Takes flights into fancy and diverts the individual from the present task.

2. Warns the individual of dangers or impending doom if he or she proceeds with the present task.

3. Raises questions about the individual's abilities or judgment, calling upon past history to support its warnings.

The left hemisphere must order the right hemisphere to stop its destructive interference, countering if it must with the realities: (1) the facts as to abilities and judgment; (2) the separating of past and present; and (3) confidence in change that has occurred through growth and experience.

If the right hemisphere persists, the individual needs to stop what he or she is doing and turn to something else. Doing so stops the flow of energy from right to left hemisphere. If this technique is repeated often enough, the neural connections that carry that energy may actually atrophy. The change in activity does not have to be drastic. For example, if you are driving a car, try to change the route you are taking. Or change the radio channel to which you are listening. The principle behind this technique is that the brain can concentrate on only one thing at a time, and a change in concentration cuts off the flow of energy. Individuals who have used this approach find that they rarely have to use it more than once. Just reminding the brain of the facts or ordering it to "concentrate" is enough to achieve the change.

Mel provides an excellent case in point.

Bright, multitalented Mel, age thirty-five, is unemployed. His waking hours, which become shorter and shorter, are occupied planning for the time when the industry will again flourish and he can begin to bring to fruition his dreams of the ideal community. His plans are based on technical knowledge and on projections of the changes imminent in society. They are innovative. They reflect his concerns for human well-being. They are not for now. No dilemma. Just inertia. Mel lives each day hoping it will be the one that signals the breakthrough.

Two models reflect Mel's pattern: the millionaire who was able to put his dreams to work and the patient dreamer who waited for the time when his dreams would be in demand. There was reason for Mel to believe that things would just "happen." He had been a very talented child. Minimal effort brought accolades from parents, teachers, and friends. He had no idea what he had done that was so exceptional. He didn't feel he had "done" anything. In his mind there had been no connection established between what he had done and what he had achieved. Magical power in operation. Magical power, one of the most firmly entrenched, more highly cherished fantasies of the right hemisphere.

What were the realities?

The realities were that Mel was married. The youngest of his three children was just six months old. There was no income. A small amount of credit was still available, but Mel's wife was most uncomfortable with deficit financing. She was considering going to work, but her skills were limited. Her earnings would be barely enough to pay for child care.

There was another reality to which Mel had to address himself: with the current state of the economy it was not likely that the type of work he had in mind would be available in the near future. In the light of this reality, which seemed beyond question, what course of action was possible? There were options. The family could go on welfare. That would require a drastic change in their life style. His wife could go home to her parents with the children and Mel could go home to his. That would place the marriage in jeopardy. Mel knew he should get a job. Mel knew he could get a job but he "couldn't."

Mel couldn't get up in the morning. He wanted only to sleep. When he did get up he was angry—not angry at anything, just angry. He had good intentions. Each day he planned what he was to do. His plans were realistic. They were appropriate, but he couldn't carry them out. His mind kept wandering to his plans for the future: the boat he would buy; the trips he and the family would take; the next house he would build with a tennis court and swimming pool.

There were some crucial questions that had to be asked.

Did Mel want to maintain this family? Did Mel want to maintain this family enough to be willing to give up the pleasures that his right hemisphere was providing for him? Was he willing to delegate to his left hemisphere the power and the authority to exercise control over right hemisphere activity?

If the answers were in the affirmative, the next steps were simple. They would, however, require discipline, full commitment, and practice. They would mean that Mel would have to give up certain of his most preferred activities. It was urgent that Mel be clear as to what we were about. We were going to change the organization of Mel's brain so that centrality would be shifted from the right hemisphere to the left hemisphere. We were going to have to make sure, for instance, that the neural network was adequate for Mel to accept becoming an employee instead of being his own boss.

To shift control from the right hemisphere to the left was first of all a matter of nurturance. Mel had to stop feeding the right hemisphere while increasing nourishment to the left hemisphere. An avid reader, science fiction was for Mel an addiction. But science fiction was a major source of nurturance for the right hemisphere, and therefore it would have to go. Mel had to be clear. We were not talking about a "forever" prohibition, only about a "for now" prohibition. How long it would have to be in effect would depend on how long it would take for the left hemisphere to gain control and enlist the right hemisphere as its ally instead of its enemy. Until that time nonfiction would have to be his exclusive reading diet: philosophy, sociology (not psychology), economics, anthropology, history. He would have to content himself with these areas until the left hemisphere had acquired the substantive knowledge it needed to assess reality and time and to exercise reason, logic, and judgment. Much of this knowledge was already stashed away in the left hemisphere. It required only activation and application. It had been several years since Mel had been engaged in systematic learning, however, and he didn't have a degree. And because of the rapid rate and scope of change taking place in the world, the knowledge stored in Mel's left hemisphere needed updating and adding to.

The next steps Mel had to pursue were equally simple. They involved:

> Taking an inventory of his knowledge and skills. What did he have to sell an employer?
>
> Taking an inventory of his experience—work, community, personal.
>
> Clarifying his preferences. What activities gave him the greatest satisfaction and sense of achievement?

This exploration would provide the raw material, the knowledge the left hemisphere needed to have about Mel as it began to chart the course of action appropriate for him at this time under the current circumstances. This self-inventory would also provide clues to the values, priorities, and goals to which the left hemisphere could look for guidance.

> One week of the reading regimen brought surprising results. Mel found that nonfiction reading was as exciting as reading science fiction, perhaps more so. And there was a plus. Science fiction often created an out-of-body, out-of-the-world feeling that caused Mel to

worry. He had studied enough psychology to know about psychoses. He worried whether he would be able to get back to "himself" after reading science fiction. Would he be able to re-enter the real world? It was a great relief to find equal pleasure with none of the risk. Mel was grateful.

In the week that Mel experimented with the new reading regimen, he also began the self-inventory. He had forgotten how venturesome he had been as an adolescent and the many varied skills he had taken the opportunity to develop. He was not yet ready to apply for a job, but he was well on the way to knowing what he would have to offer an employer. He thought he might even soon be able to make at least a beginning determination of the kind of work he would prefer.

To make a conscious commitment to left hemisphere control of brain activity and brain power is no simple decision. It is much easier to operate according to nature's preprogrammed design. This preset design is extensive and quite exquisite. Take the bee. With a brain so small the sharpest of pencil points is too large to draw it, the bee engages in many finely discriminating tasks. The same holds for ants and flies, birds and fish. Much can be done and enjoyed with what nature has provided. One does not need to bring experience under the psychological microscope of consciously defined values, priorities, and goals. One does not have to subject what nature has provided to the influence of knowledge, reason, judgment, and logic. One can even acquire knowledge at the highest levels of cognitive effort and not use it. One can store it away much as people store away in safety deposit boxes their precious jewels, never to be used, never to be enjoyed.

Donna was clear. She knew she had a choice. Her choice was beyond question.

A resort pool was the place. The summer of 1981 was the time. Donna had just flown in from the East for a series of treatments to supplement her psychotherapy. I was a long way from home too, attending a conference of social psychotherapists. How natural, an in-depth conversation about the human estate.

Donna was fascinated by my neural network approach to change. She knew about the hemispheres. Her therapist used a similar approach. She didn't always like it. It did not take Donna long to come to a conclusion: she would never have me as her therapist. I was too cognitive, too intellectual. She would never turn over to knowledge, logic, and reason the management of her life. She wanted a "gut" feeling about her life.

How quick she had been to spot the incompatibility in our goals. She was bright. She was multitalented. All she wanted was "every-thing." She did not concern herself with what was possible. She was giving little more than lip service to the warning signals of her body. She didn't recognize or acknowledge limitations. She was at risk in the most crucial sense. She knew it but paid no attention. She wanted what she wanted. She was not willing to concern herself with whether what she wanted was available or not.

Requisites for Change

In order to consider, venture, and achieve change one must be dissatisfied—not necessarily unhappy, just restless, wanting something more or something different. The next step needs to be either (1) figuring out the nature of the dissatis-faction or the source of it to determine whether change is necessary, possible, or desired; or (2) identifying the source of the restlessness: what one would want more of, what one might want different. In this search, one needs to bring into play one's values, priorities, and goals; whatever one has of a philosophy of life; whatever one might have of a view of what one would like one's life to be.

Values, priorities, and goals are our guidelines. They help us chart our course. They help keep us on the course we

have charted and aid us should a change of course be under
consideration.

Ms. D. was distressed. She could not go on in so disorganized a way,
without purpose; without direction. Her job as a parent would just
about come to an end when her youngest child left for college in six
months. Her husband was totally immersed in his many projects,
each of which he loved. Ms. D. had lived her life as a parent fully
involved in the many things that responsible parenthood required.
She had always been available to do what needed to be done, and
she had enjoyed it all, though she dismissed it as insignificant.

Ms. D. had even found time to pursue some additional education.
She had dabbled in art and music, enjoying it and doing well. None
of her activities or interests, however, added up to a feeling of
accomplishment. It all seemed so futile.

Ms. D. saw herself as undisciplined and self-indulgent—a dilet-
tante. She didn't want to be that way. She wanted to be accomplished. She wanted to make a "difference." But every time she set
out to do that there seemed to be a thin but persistent voice that
said: "You don't want to do that." "You can't." Or even occasionally: "You don't dare." And sure enough, she would manage somehow to scuttle what she had undertaken to do. She hadn't even
been able to stop smoking. Something as simple as that.

A review of Ms. D.'s many activities and interests established
beyond any doubt that she was a bright, talented, and energetic
individual with tremendous capacity for commitment. Her values,
too, were clear and firm. What was not clear was her "right" to be
who she was. All her life, from as far back as age three, she had tried
hard to be what other people wanted her to be. Her most vivid
childhood memory was trying desperately to be the son her father
had wanted. In adulthood this effort translated into trying to be as
expert as her husband in his chosen field.

Four interviews and Ms. D. was clear. She knew which section of
the brain was giving her difficulty. She knew the issues. She suddenly
knew her rights. For the first time in her forty-five years she felt in
control of her life. She was sure her old pattern of operation would
end.Evidence was already present. She had withdrawn from the
course she had started that was not in the field of her interests. She

really didn't have to worry about finances and she wasn't going to. She was going to let her husband have the pleasure of supporting the family in the way he wanted to. Their relationship was already much improved. She was appreciating him for what he was able to do and just not "fussing" about what did not come naturally or easily. For the first time in their twenty-three-year marriage she was really seeing him as the individual he was and had the right to be—an individual just as she is an individual.

Rights, options, pattern of operation—these had to be examined. In addition, there was reality—what could be changed, what had to be accepted "as is." There was also cost to consider. What would be involved for Ms. D. and for the others in her life if she undertook to do what she wanted to do, whatever that might be? The soul searching Ms. D. did between interviews was extensive. Her head was literally in a whirl. But it was exciting, because for the first time she was beginning to see and understand herself, her husband, and her children. Only now was she beginning to realize what a hard time she had given her family all these years, all because of something that was completely beyond their control. She was sorry. But until now it had been beyond her control also. She would have to forgive herself.

Furrowing Mental Soil

"If you haven't had a new idea or discarded an old one recently, check," advised a personality theorist, "you may be dead." I'm not sure I agree. The issue is not whether one is dead but rather to what extent one is alive. To be alive implies being active, being involved, experiencing, and changing.

Just as the soil crusts, so does the brain. In addition to the natural encrusting, the loyalty to what we know, think, and believe, there is the limbic section, the oldest section of the brain that exerts all of the power it can muster to keep us anchored to habit and tradition. It is a devotee of the law of gravity or inertia. Its resistance to change is intense. It is content with the neural network nature predesigned. It will protect itself in whatever ways it can from the intrusions of reality, knowledge, judgment, and logic which threaten the serenity and security of its domain.

To undertake change in the face of this two-pronged resistance requires conscious determination, active procedures and practice. If we decide to learn to play a musical instrument, we accept without question the need to practice very simple scales over and over again to achieve proficiency. The same is necessary if one wants to convert one's brain from operating according to preset instinct, reflex, and habit to operating according to substantive knowledge, logic, and judgment. The conversion is specific. It involves conscious thinking instead of unconscious, intuitive knowledge and wisdom accumulated without conscious intent or effort. It is there. One uses it.

To convert from the intuitive to the conscious, from instinct to reason, is not likely to occur by chance or by an evolutionary leap. It is a task which must be undertaken consciously and deliberately, with full realization of consequence. The task is difficult, but it is achievable. It involves choice. It requires commitment. Three steps will lead the way.

1. Make a list of your pet ideas.
2. Prove each of them wrong.
3. Consider how many other ways the issues might be viewed.

This exercise exposes your brain to new perceptions, new points of view, and different values. In the end you may arrive back where you started, but it will be with greater clarity and conviction, expanded horizons, and some new equipment for understanding the views of others. You may find that your range of knowledge is inadequate to engage the above exercise fully. The library is a vast gold mine for expanding one's intellectual resources and one's awareness of the ever-expanding opportunities that a world in the throes of massive change presents.

Points to Ponder

Why it is necessary for the limbic section to be educated while it is sufficient for the right hemisphere only to be controlled we can only conjecture with our current level of knowledge. The human organism probably can function reasonably well under most circumstances without imagination, without wings. The right hemisphere, therefore, can be left to its own devices as long as it does not interfere with left hemisphere functioning. Perhaps the limbic section as the source of feelings that affect action and as the area in which the life-sustaining systems are located (circulation, respiration, appetite) is more crucial to an adequately functioning human organism.

What is becoming abundantly clear is that if the archaic emotions of the limbic section are not brought under rational control, the human species is not likely to survive. Our technical sophistication requires the very highest level of knowledge, logic, and judgment if the human estate is to continue and be viable.

The realities we face in dealing with the limbic section are manifold.

The limbic section is essential to human well-being and survival.

The limbic section is uneducated but educable.

The neural connections between the limbic section and the left hemisphere, the source of knowledge, are sparse or nonexistent.

We know very little about the content and the processing pattern of the limbic section. Thanks to psychoanalysis we know much more about the right hemisphere, and consequently can move more surely in bringing it into harmony with the other sections of the brain.

Another aspect of the challenge we face is the question of left hemisphere competence to deal with the limbic section. Since we know so little about limbic section functioning, the left hemisphere must take responsibility for determining the information the limbic section needs to function appropriately in our electronic world. This is a tremendous responsibility. And there are people like Donna, who say *never* would they turn final authority over to knowledge, logic, reason, and judgment. She wants to live life at the "gut" level. That is a decision each human being is privileged to make. As a society and as a world we need only to make sure that the persons who are in positions of power and authority over others are ruled by knowledge, logic, reason, and judgment. The latter must be under the aegis of justice and compassion, with a good measure of humility thrown in. Instinct, reflex, and habit are not adequate to the task.

As one considers invasion into the limbic section so that it can become a fully active member of the brain/mind complex, one must be sure the executive "I" understands the process and the goals. The executive "I" tends to worry. If the limbic section is brought under conscious control, will we become unfeeling people? If we bring the right hemisphere under conscious control and within the bounds of reality, will we destroy creativity? The answer on both scores is a firm and confident *no*. What is to the good of the human organism as a whole is not destroyed. In fact, it is expanded and freed. Knowing the law of gravity did not keep us from going to the moon and back. Knowing the law of magnetism did not keep us from developing radio, television, and now communications satellites. There may be times when the human organism, like the centipede, is immobilized:

The centipede had no trouble running
Until the toad in fun
Asked him which foot came after which.
Whereupon he lay immobilized in the ditch.

With the human being, any immobilization would be only temporary. Knowing "which foot comes after which" adds to our power to be truly in the driver's seat of our lives, the true artists of the masterpieces we would like our lives to be.

Summary

In the organization and design of the human brain lies the hope and the promise of the human species. The possibility exists that the neural network can be expanded geometrically or more as it is developed. The 10 billion neurons that make up the brain pose unlimited possibilities if the brain is in position and in condition to "spin free," expanding the network that already exists and developing new networks and new connections with the long established and the newly developed. [12] Essential to mind development is knowledge and awareness of how one's particular mind functions. Another prerequisite is that one must have confidence in one's brain. This confidence must extend to allowing one's brain to be tired, even to "go on strike" if it has been overworked or under stress.

Confidence of this quality is possible only if one can acknowledge and accept the nature of brain functioning. The brain must have time and opportunity to ingest new knowledge and experience and to monitor and process it. The mind does not respond well to the dogmatic or autocratic approach, to "musts." It abhors self-criticism. It is immobilized by self-doubt and discouragement. It can be destroyed by boredom. It takes on wings when self-confidence is high.

There are conditions, both internal and external, that provide optimum opportunity for brain and mind development. There are also internal and external conditions that thwart optimal development. To know these conditions is to know one's mind and to be in control of its functioning.

CHAPTER **6**

A New Agenda

It doesn't matter where you've been
Or how you happened where you are.
All you need to know
Is where you want to go.

Essentially, this was the message of a courageous, innovative group of practitioners in the 1930s and 1940s who tried hard to break the hold of history on individual destiny. They replaced Freud's recapitulation theory (that you had to relive trauma in order to expurgate its ill effects) with a focus on the importance of the here and now and belief in the power of the individual will.

The neural network approach to brain organization and design brings into sharp focus the "here and now"—who are you—and the power of the will—what would you like to make of your life. The questions are not philosophical. They are not utopian. They are real and they are urgent. These questions spell the difference between being alive as long as one lives or fossilizing, becoming at best a relic of what has been.

Anthropologists point out that species survive because they adapt. They do not adapt in order to survive. This implies a response to change that is spontaneous, not premeditated. It suggests a sensitivity to change and a flexibility more intuitive than reasoned. It requires a readiness to alter and accommodate.

As we bring into the range of our conscious vision the brain as the remarkable organ that it is, we can begin to realize that we have within our native-born equipment potential far beyond our logical comprehension. It is impossible for us to imagine what the billions of brain cells connected by trillions of neural fibers could do if they were properly connected and directed. Some scientists estimate that every individual has a potential I.Q. of 130, which is genius category according to our current system of measurement. Possibly our emerging electronic, computerized, miniaturized world will require entirely different neural connections and differently equipped brain cells than those that have been brought into play by industrialization. Certainly children who are growing up today on a recreational diet of electronic games are going to have differently designed brains than those of us who grew up playing marbles, jacks, and hopscotch before the era of radio and television.

The world which one can circle by jet in eighty hours is very different from the horse-and-buggy world into which I was born. I was a rarity. I had been abroad three times before I was sixteen. How we marveled when we could cross the ocean in only five days instead of the usual fourteen. Today, it is almost a common experience for youngsters to take "time out" from school or work to travel, study, or work abroad. National boundaries are being bridged. New cultures, new foods, and new languages are being experienced, if not enjoyed or adopted. The "one world" Wendell Wilkie predicted in the 1940s is coming into being. Its birth is being almost precipitated by instant intercontinental communication. We are witnesses and participants, whether we wish it or not, to whatever happens anywhere. The world is our neighborhood, and every person everywhere is our neighbor.

It has been said that two children in the same family born ten years apart live in two different worlds, that persons over thirty must be resocialized. Persons born before 1920 are viewed as being the bridge between the nineteenth and twenty-first centuries. The fact that this generation has experienced so many changes gives hope that its members have the capabilities required for further change.

Change is most taxing on adults. It is they who find themselves strangers in their own land, floundering where old landmarks have disappeared, confused where familiar crossroads are bypassed. Change is easier on children. The new is the only reality they have known. They do not know that what they are experiencing is different. In a subtle way the new world is filtering in. Songs are the vehicle.

> "You're the most important person in the world to you and you hardly even know you," is the theme of a favorite children's program.
>
> "Sing a song, sing a song . . . don't worry if it's not good enough for anyone else to hear. Sing a song," is another.
>
> And then there is the "kingdom of it could be you."

Here are three messages, distinctly new. These three messages—whether intentionally or unintentionally, implicitly or explicitly—herald the new world. In a mobile world of global dimensions one is likely to find oneself where one's best friends are strangers on the move. How important it will be to have a firm sense of self—to know what one enjoys and what gives life excitement, challenge, beauty, and comfort.

How important it will be to appreciate one's own achievements. Appreciation and praise will be welcomed, but of necessity they will be the jam that flavors the bread and butter, not the bread itself. And then, in a world of ever-expanding horizons, how important it will be to have the feel of wide-open spaces, of opportunities waiting to be explored and tested.

Adults would do well to add these songs to their repertoire. The messages they carry have no age boundary. Coupled with the old favorite reminding us that the "greatest treasure on earth" is to be "young at heart," these three new songs are a beginning. They lay new cornerstones for the personality of the future.

Current Reality and Future Projections

It has been estimated that:

> In the six-year period 1967 to 1973 scientific knowledge and technology developed more than in all of history.

> In the next 30 years—1982 to 2011—we will experience changes comparable to those represented by the shift from an agricultural to an industrial society some 5,000 years ago.

> If we live until 1989, we may live in a world where there is no natural death. We will die by accident or choice. Otherwise we may be able to live forever in youth and vigor.

> Coupled with this projection is another—that we will be retired at birth.

> An electronically operated world will require relatively few people. Life without natural death and without aging will have more and more people available at a maximal level of functioning.

> Production will continue at a high level without concern for wages, sick leave, vacations, or retirement. Profits will accrue. Our problem

will be to distribute profits so that the population remains capable of consuming the products that technology will enable us to produce. But the problem is not a serious one. We already have the instruments to deal with it—unemployment compensation, social security, the beginnings of a guaranteed annual wage.

Long life without aging, extended leisure without economic want, retirement at birth: What will be the essence of living? What is the most one can expect of the life experience? We have been preprogrammed to survive. We must reprogram to "live."

Redesigning to "Live"

To Make Life "Better"

To have life that is "good" but that one wants to have "better" is a subjective matter, one of degree. Right hemisphere development may be the issue: an expansion in scope, an expansion in depth. Imagination and the sense of wonder, curiosity, and adventure are the instruments for life-quality expansion. The law of magnetism, the unexpected, the dynamic, need to be brought into play. Among the hallmarks of quality living are:

Joy without guilt

Achievement-satisfaction without apology

Zest without anxiety

Adventure without fear

These goals are achievable only if one is clear about one's rights and one's obligations to others; if one is confident of one's judgment; and if one has developed a reasonable amount of confidence in one's values, priorities, and goals. All of this implies a person in one's own right: autonomous, authentic, and upward striving, not in material things but in self-realization. An appropriate motto for the quality-seeker is the old adage: "Hitch your wagon to a star or what's a heaven for?"

It was on a rubber raft ride on the Snake River in the Grand Tetons that we met Mr. and Mrs. W. They were in their middle sixties, enjoying their second honeymoon after 40 odd years of marriage. It was good to be back enjoying old scenes. That there was a freezing rain pelting down as we sat in the open without cover didn't faze them. They were doing what they had dreamed of during the years that they were rearing their four sons. Their children were well launched into professions. Mr. W. was fortunate to have had a profession that gave him much pleasure for many years. They were financially comfortable. They could do whatever they wanted to do. Two years ago they bought a camper and set out to visit every state in the United States. Their aim was to see and experience as much as was possible, and to travel on their own was the way they wanted to do it. They were meeting interesting people wherever they went, and each stop along the way added to their wonder at the marvels of nature.

Joy and Lee had a different idea for bringing variety and new experience into their lives. Their 25-year marriage had been rich in travel. Lee's business as an exporter had brought them into contact with unusual people all over the world. They wanted nothing more than to settle down in simple surroundings. They bought a large frame house that was 150 years old which they spent two years repairing and reconstructing. They bought three beautiful horses and had a variety of livestock. For them there was something very real about living close to nature. Another dimension was added to their experience when they opened their home to a runaway boy who had sought refuge at their church. They had had no children, and this was a new and enriching experience for them.

To be free to develop in breadth and depth one must make some conscious decisions. These decisions are executive, managerial, operational:

What portion of time, energy, money will one allot, to people, to situations, to things, to new experiences?

What takes precedence over what?

To whom is one accountable?

These decisions require a firm sense of self and one's rights. They require confidence in one's judgment. They require commitment to a set of values that contribute to one's sense of purpose and to one's self-esteem.

To Have Life Be Different

To set out on a new road is intrinsically more difficult than adding quality to the road that is already established and well traveled. To some people attempting the new comes naturally. If there is a mountain to be climbed, they want to climb it. If there is a cave to be explored, they want to explore it. If there is a sea to be plumbed, they want to plumb it. They are the ones who have charted new roads. It is probably from among them that have come the 1,000 individuals who have made possible the world we are experiencing and having to adjust to today. To such individuals change is challenge. They welcome it.

To those of us to whom change does not come naturally or easily, the emerging world poses a dilemma. The world we have known and for which we have been prepared by education and experience has about spent its course. We have a choice. We can become the relics of the world that has been. We can become a part of the world that is being born.

To become a part of the new world may involve rediscovery—of interests and of talents that have always existed but have been sidestepped for others. It may involve discovery, even invention—becoming aware of interests and talents one did not know one had, or inventing new talents and interests where none have existed. Discovery and invention both require an inventory:

What one would like.

What one would like to become.

What is necessary to achieve what one would like to become.

What resources are available, physical, psychological, social, economic.

Are the resources adequate to the task?

If the resources are inadequate to the task, can they be increased; or do goals have to be modified in the light of available resources?

Discovery and invention are left hemisphere enterprises. They deal with realities: what is; what can be; and how what can be may be achieved.

Theda wanted urgently to be bright, knowledgeable, vivacious, spontaneous. She tried hard to emulate many "models" among her friends. She couldn't. Her protest was of long standing. It was urgent. There was almost a desperation about it. Theda was advised that there were some things she could do to check out whether she had the capability to be what she said she wanted to be. It would take approximately three months of following a specified regimen before we would know. Theda was willing, in fact eager, to try.

The first step involved approximately five hours a week for two weeks at the library, just browsing randomly to see what subjects intrigued her mind. The next step required that the same amount of time be spent skimming an area that interested her. Finally, Theda was to move on to a program of reading in the subject that interested her most. The five hours allocated for each step throughout the period would be a constant, a minimum. If after the initial browsing period she found more time available and wanted to spend it on the project, fine.

What we would be doing was first checking out Theda's areas of interest. The second step would be checking her reading skills and determining whether there was anything amiss in her reading pattern (this was suspected). Theda was assured that there were techniques for correcting a problem if one existed.

A two-week period was allotted for the first step of browsing. Theda was able to follow the plan for only one week, and only sporadically. She did not return.

Theda's wants were clear, and she had nursed them her whole life. She wanted to be rid of them by autocratic ruling (I want things different) rather than by consistent, disciplined effort. What she wanted was not attainable on her terms. She was wanting by instinct, reflex, and habit what was available only by conscious, deliberate effort.

Stanley's situation was different. His wanting was not elective. Life had shattered his world. He could pick up the pieces and construct a facsimile of what he had had. But it would be only a facsimile, and he wasn't sure he wanted only an approximation of what he had already had for 40 years.

Stanley's marriage of 40 years ended abruptly with Heda's sudden death. Heda had been Stanley's world. She had planned, directed, and managed all the details of a large business and a busy household. Stanley had been the implementer, but always under direction.

Unlike the young Indian who lost his way in the woods, Stanley was not able to square his shoulders and with head high say: "Me not lost. Wigwam lost." Stanley was as lost as any adult human being could be. And there was no wigwam.

Finances were no problem. Heda had managed well. Stanley could do anything he wanted to do. What did he want to do? What an overwhelming question that was! He didn't know where to start. He didn't know who "he" was. He had no idea what his interests, aptitudes, or preferences were. He had been a pawn on a chessboard, moving where and when moving was required.

After a period of random reading in the library and attendance at a number of classes and workshops, Stanley became aware of an interest in law—not a burning interest, but an interest, nonetheless. He remembered fondly his many business conferences with attorneys. He made a decision. He began to explore the possibility of law as a career. He had made a beginning in self-discovery, a beginning in inventing a new future for himself.

The concept of lifelong learning has developed in our society only in very recent years. Like the idea of recycling, or retooling, it has burgeoned. One hears more and more often of adults who venture into new professions or who go back to school to expand their knowledge and their skills. Some stay within the range of their dominant hemisphere— accountants who become attorneys (left hemisphere); artists who become musicians (right hemisphere); educators who become counselors or therapists (limbic section). Others venture into new areas of their brain—surgeons who become artists (a shift from left hemisphere to right); therapists who become computer programmers (limbic section to left hemisphere); novelists who become nonfiction writers (limbic section to left hemisphere in content). Writing itself is a left hemisphere activity.

College youth today is inclining toward multidisciplinary training. Whether by instinct or analysis, they are preparing for a fluid world in the throes of rapid and massive social change. Long life in good health and youthful vigor will be conditioned primarily by the range of one's interests and the options one chooses. Life can be:

An unfolding mystery

An unending adventure

A magnet to the stars.

Addendum

The neural fibers so compactly encased in our brains if placed end to end would reach to the moon and back, so estimate some brain researchers. This idea is beyond our comprehension, to be sure. But there is in this estimate, even if it is exaggerated, the suggestion that virtually anything that human beings may desire is possible. Placed in juxtaposition with the idea that perhaps life's purpose must be created, not discovered, one finds oneself truly in harmony with nature, partners in the eternal search for:

Questions that need to be answered.
Answers that need to be questioned.

This is the ultimate challenge vested by nature in the human estate.

References

1. Calder, Nigel, *The Mind of Man* (New York: Viking Press, 1970), p. 29.
2. Cloud, Preston, *Cosmos, Earth and Man* (New Haven, Conn.: Yale University Press, 1978), p. 220.
3. Russell, Peter, *The Brain Book* (New York: Hawthorne Books, Inc., 1979), p. 166.
4. Rand McNally, *Atlas of Body and Mind* (New York: Rand McNally, 1978), pp. 116–121.
5. Jaynes, Julian, *The Origin of Consciousness and the Breakdown of the Bicameral Brain* (Boston: Houghton Mifflin, 1976), pp. 307–313, 325.
6. Wolman, Benjamin J., ed., *International Encyclopedia of Psychiatry, Psychology and Neurology*, (New York: Nostrand Reinhold Company, 1977), Vol. 10, pp. 401–430.
7. Gardner, Howard, "Strange Loops of the Mind," *Psychology Today*, March 1980, pp. 78–79.
8. Fergusson, Marilyn, *The Brain Revolution* (New York: Taplinger Publishing Company, 1975), pp. 182–183.
9. Janov, Arthur, *Primal Man, the New Consciousness* (New York: Thomas Y. Crowell Company, 1975), p. 46.
10. Fergusson, Marilyn, *The Aquarian Conspiracy* (New York: J.P. Tarcher, Inc., 1980), pp. 23–29.
11. Blakemore, Colin, *Mechanics of the Mind* (Cambridge, England: Cambridge University Press, 1977), p. 45.
12. Glasser, William, *Positive Addiction* (New York: Harper & Row Publishers, Inc., 1976).

Bibliography

Bronowski, J. *The Ascent of Man*. Boston: Little, Brown and Company, 1973.
Casidy, Harold G. *Science Re-Stated*. San Francisco: Freeman, Cooper, 1970.
Heisenberg, Werner. *Across the Frontier*. New York: Harper & Row Publishers, Inc., 1974.
Restak, Richard M. *The Brain: The Last Frontier*. New York: Doubleday & Company, Inc., 1979.
Rose, Steven. *The Conscious Brain*. New York: Alfred A. Knopf, Inc., 1973.
Rosenfeld, Albert, ed. *Mind and Super-Mind*. New York: Holt, Rinehart and Winston, 1977.
Sagan, Carl. *Dragons of Eden*. New York: Random House, Inc., 1977.
Trefil, James S. *From Atoms to Quarks*. New York: Charles Scribners' Sons, Inc., 1980.
Young, J.Z. *Programs of the Brain*. Oxford, England: Oxford University Press, 1978.